EL
CÓMIC
NO. 1
Pop-ojo
I WILL BUILD A GREAT WALL -- AND NOBODY BUILDS WALLS BETTER THAN ME, BELIEVE ME --
OJO

EL CÓMIC
JUNE
NO. 1
Still 10¢
Señor Gonzales
?
WHEN MEXICO SENDS ITS PEOPLE, THEY'RE NOT SENDING THEIR BEST....
THEY'RE BRINGING DRUGS. THEY'RE BRINGING CRIME. THEY'RE RAPISTS. AND SOME, I ASSUME, ARE GOOD PEOPLE.

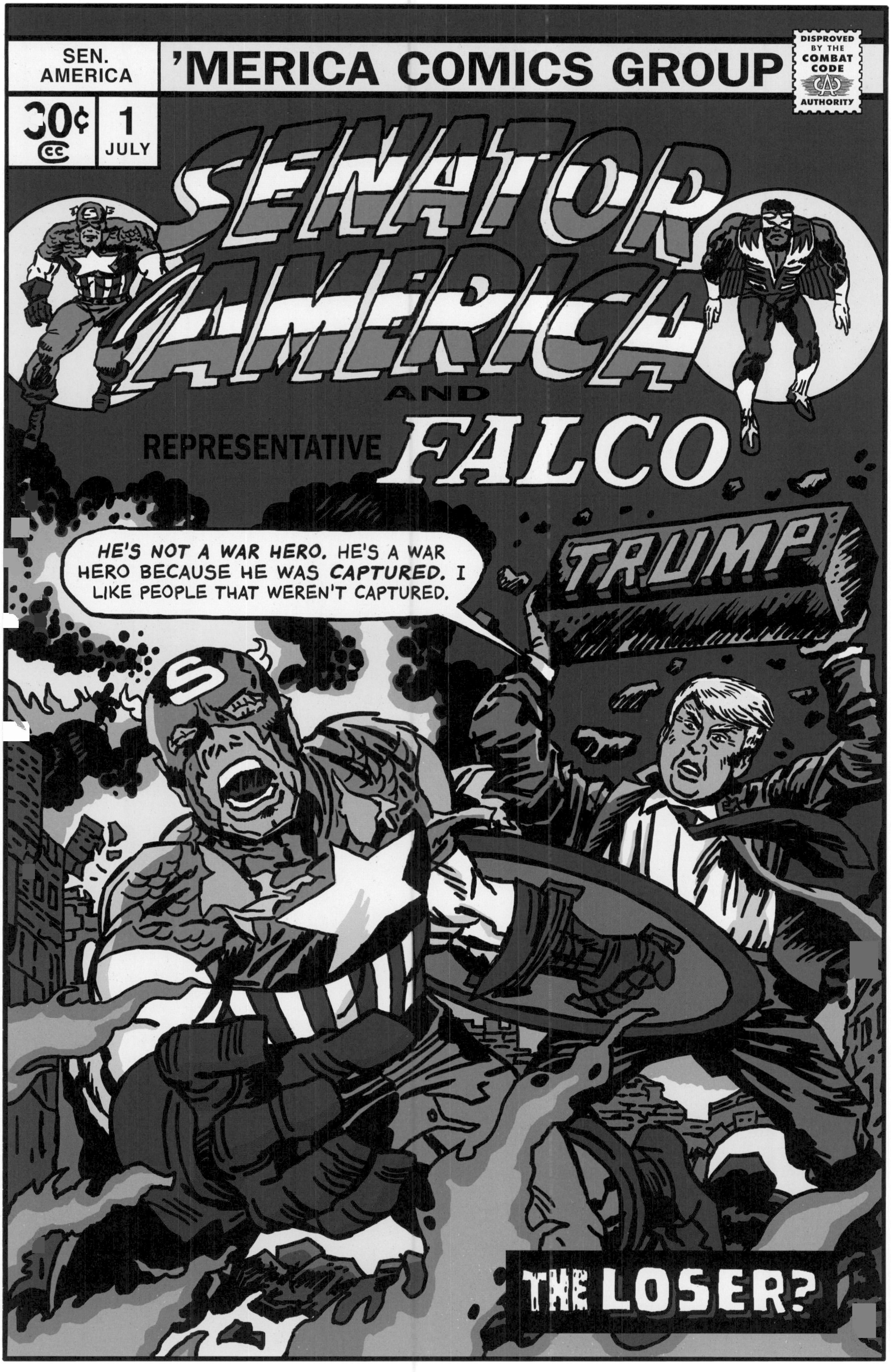
SEN. AMERICA
'MERICA COMICS GROUP
DISPROVED BY THE COMBAT CODE AUTHORITY
30¢ CC
1 JULY
SENATOR AMERICA
AND
REPRESENTATIVE FALCO
HE'S NOT A WAR HERO. HE'S A WAR HERO BECAUSE HE WAS CAPTURED. I LIKE PEOPLE THAT WEREN'T CAPTURED.
TRUMP
THE LOSER?

'MERICA COMICS
RICH GUYS IN DISGUISE
TRUMPS FORMERS
GENERALIZATION 1
$1.75 USA
1
JULY
CC 72015
ACKNOWLEDGED BY THE COLD COMFORT AUTHORITY
I AM MORE FOR THE MILITARY... I AM THE MOST MILITARISTIC PERSON IN THIS ROOM. I WOULD HAVE A MILITARY THAT IS SO STRONG THAT WE WOULD NEVER HAVE TO USE IT. BECAUSE PEOPLE WOULD SAY, "NO WAY WE'RE MESSING WITH THEM...!"

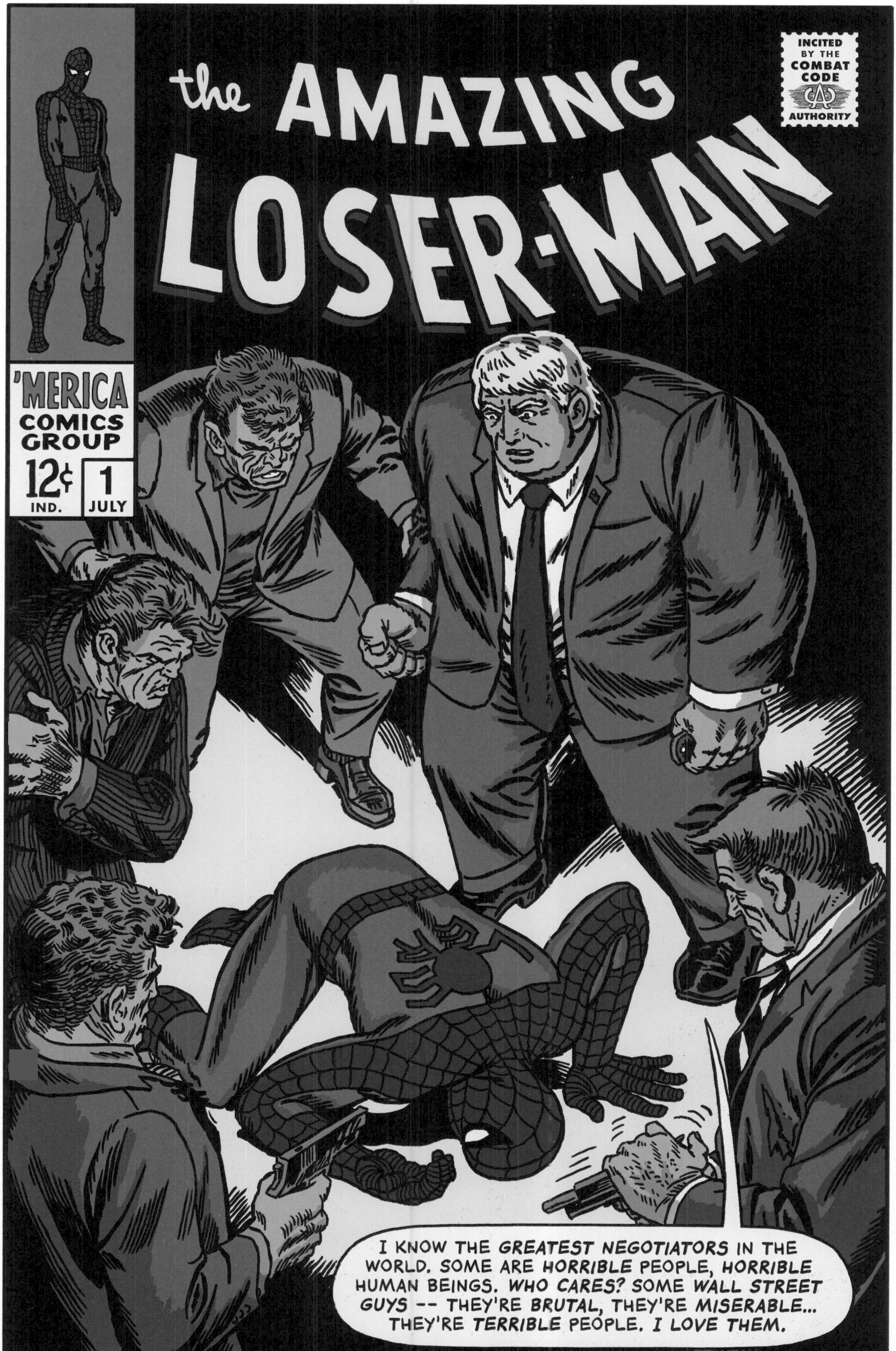

the AMAZING
LOSER-MAN
INCITED BY THE COMBAT CODE AUTHORITY
'MERICA COMICS GROUP
12¢ IND.
1 JULY
I KNOW THE *GREATEST NEGOTIATORS* IN THE WORLD. SOME ARE *HORRIBLE* PEOPLE, *HORRIBLE* HUMAN BEINGS. *WHO CARES?* SOME *WALL STREET GUYS* -- THEY'RE *BRUTAL*, THEY'RE *MISERABLE*... THEY'RE *TERRIBLE* PEOPLE. *I LOVE THEM.*

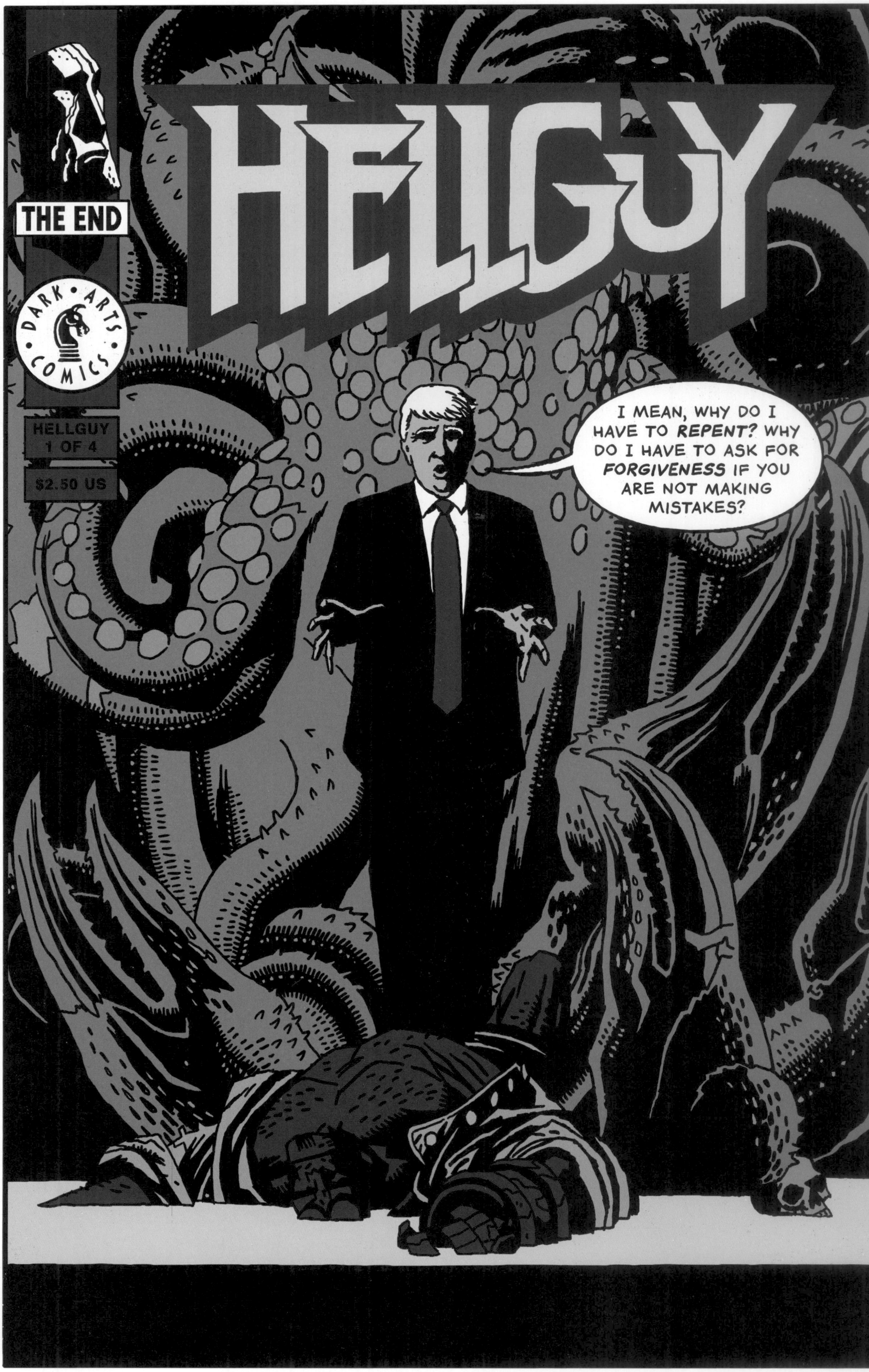
HELLGUY
THE END
DARK ARTS COMICS
HELLGUY 1 OF 4
$2.50 US
I MEAN, WHY DO I HAVE TO REPENT? WHY DO I HAVE TO ASK FOR FORGIVENESS IF YOU ARE NOT MAKING MISTAKES?

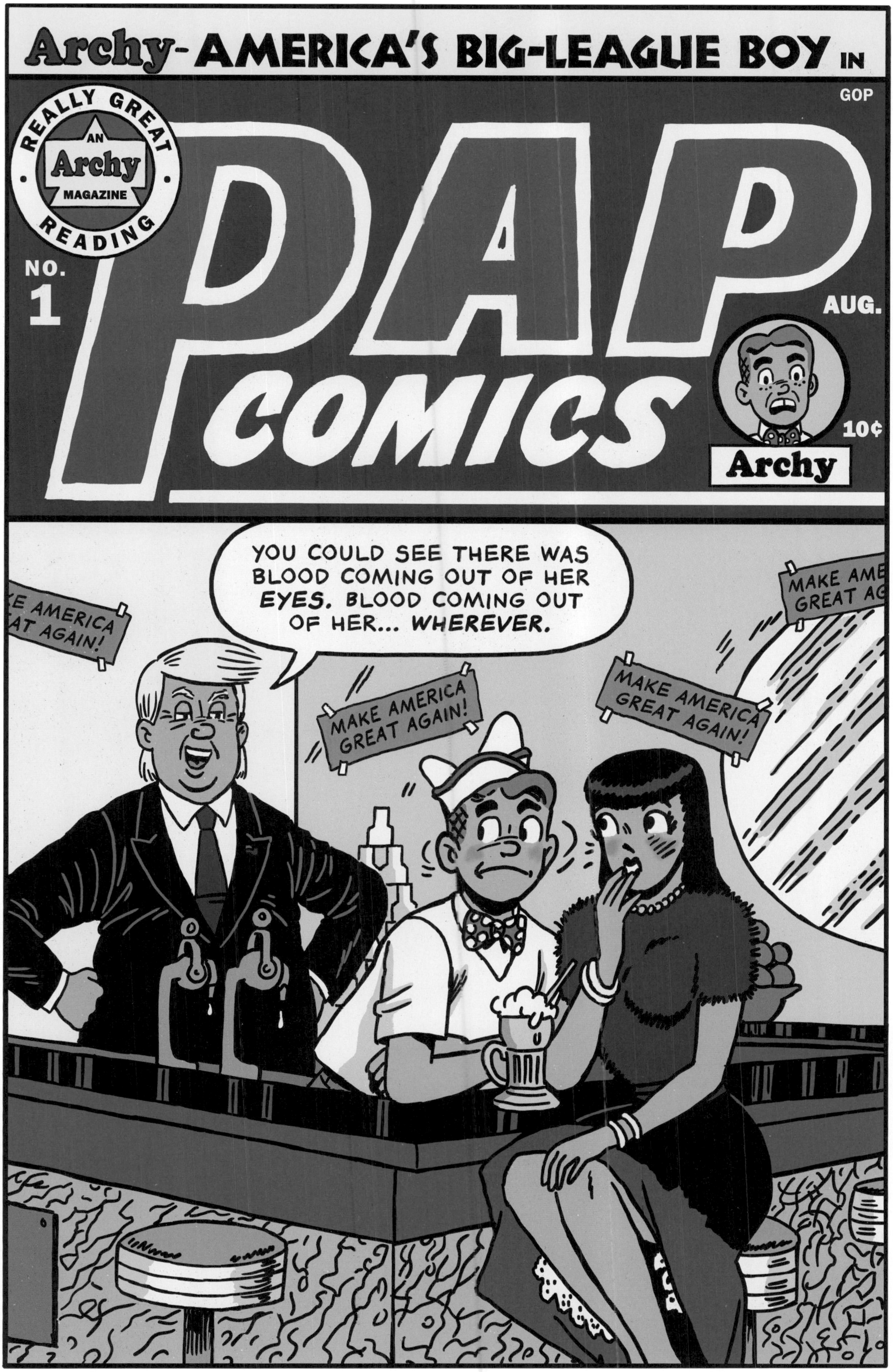

Archy-AMERICA'S BIG-LEAGUE BOY IN
GOP
REALLY GREAT AN Archy MAGAZINE READING
PAP COMICS
NO. 1
AUG.
10¢
Archy
YOU COULD SEE THERE WAS BLOOD COMING OUT OF HER EYES. BLOOD COMING OUT OF HER... WHEREVER.
MAKE AMERICA GREAT AGAIN!
MAKE AMERICA GREAT AGAIN!
MAKE AMERICA GREAT AGAIN!

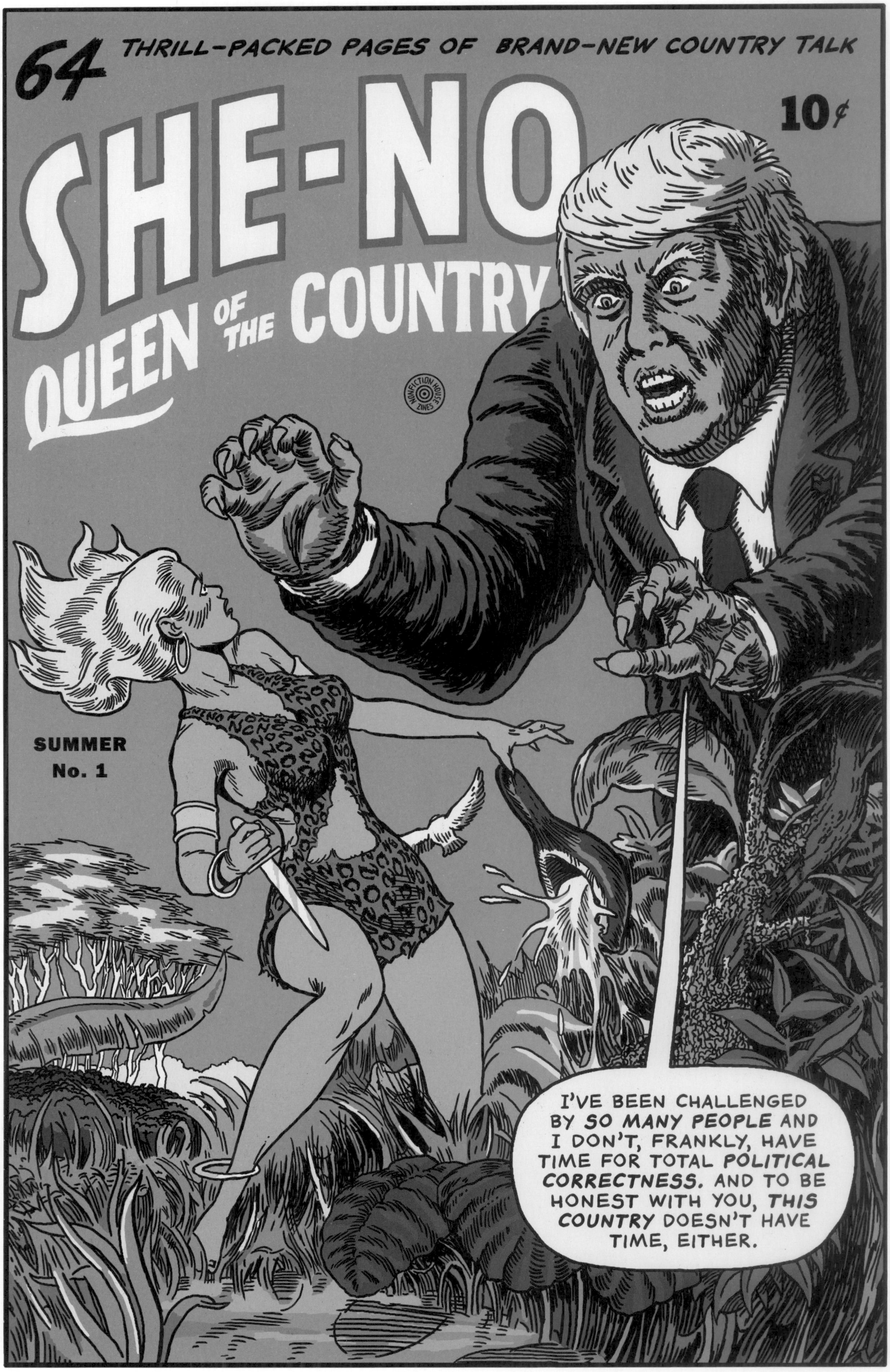
64 THRILL-PACKED PAGES OF BRAND-NEW COUNTRY TALK
10¢
SHE-NO
QUEEN OF THE COUNTRY
SUMMER
No. 1
I'VE BEEN CHALLENGED BY SO MANY PEOPLE AND I DON'T, FRANKLY, HAVE TIME FOR TOTAL POLITICAL CORRECTNESS. AND TO BE HONEST WITH YOU, THIS COUNTRY DOESN'T HAVE TIME, EITHER.

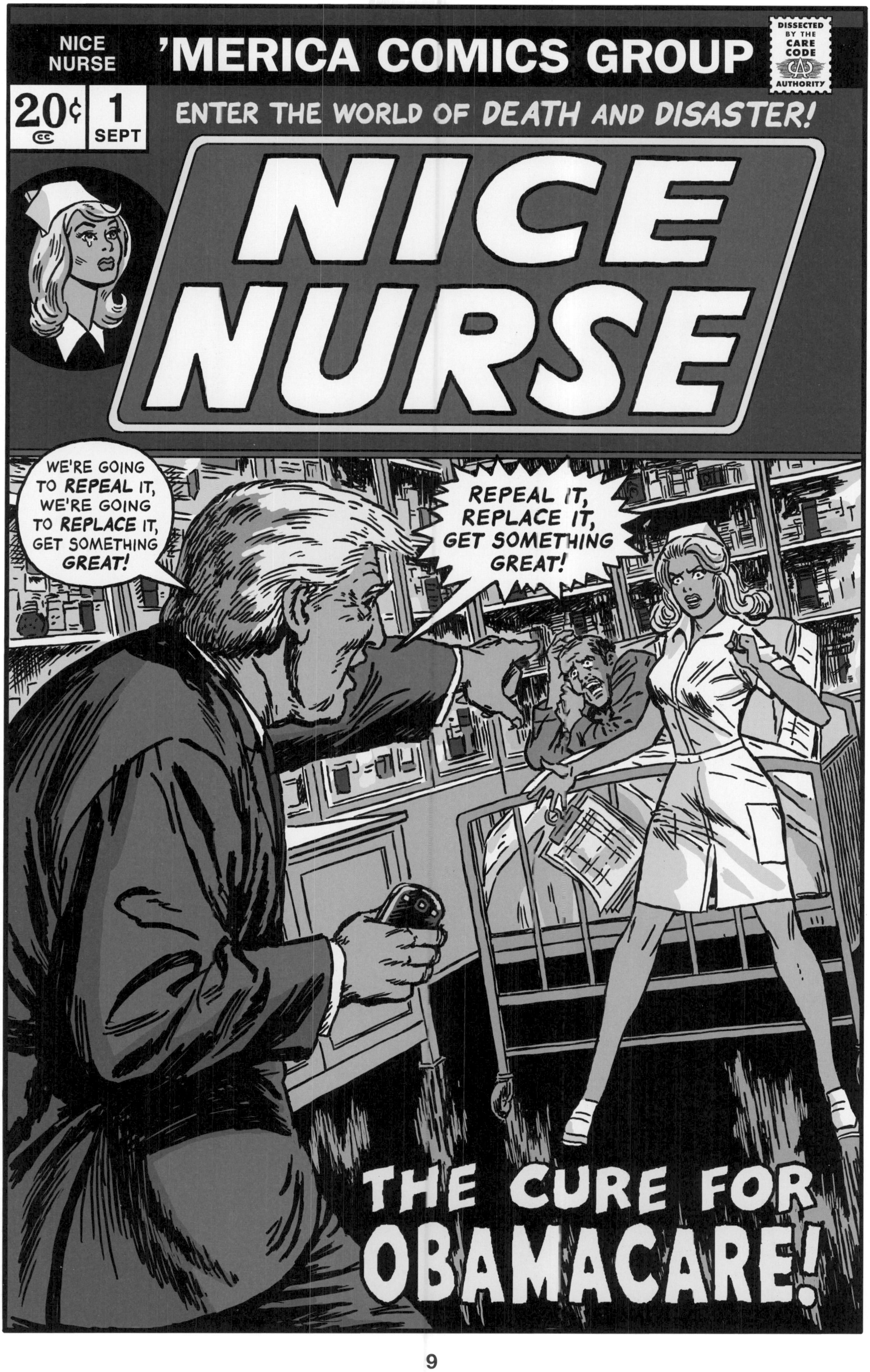
NICE NURSE
'MERICA COMICS GROUP
DISSECTED BY THE CARE CODE AUTHORITY
20¢
1 SEPT
ENTER THE WORLD OF DEATH AND DISASTER!
NICE NURSE
WE'RE GOING TO REPEAL IT, WE'RE GOING TO REPLACE IT, GET SOMETHING GREAT!
REPEAL IT, REPLACE IT, GET SOMETHING GREAT!
THE CURE FOR OBAMACARE!

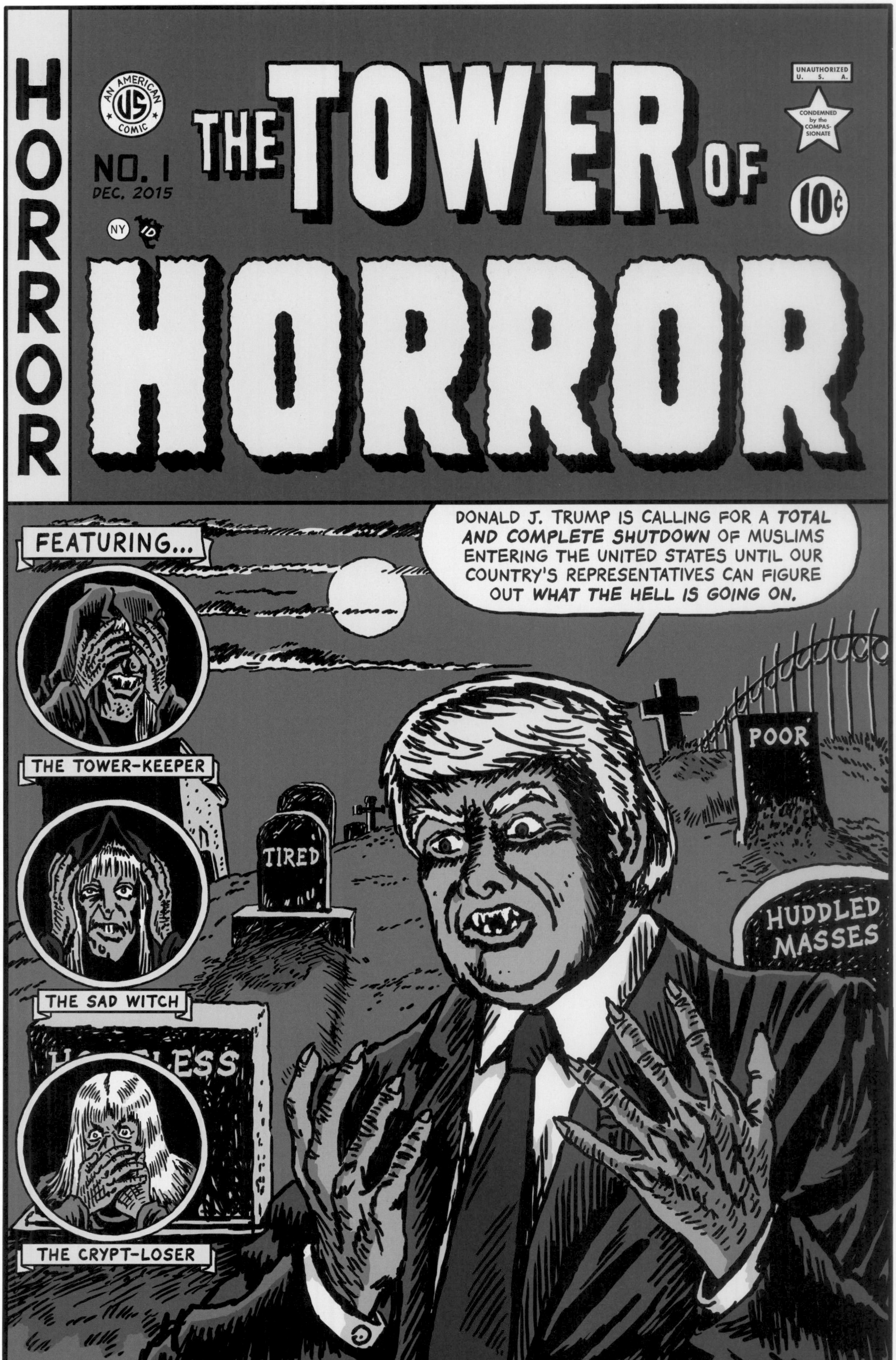
HORROR
AN AMERICAN US COMIC
NO. 1
DEC. 2015
NY ID
THE TOWER OF
HORROR
UNAUTHORIZED U. S. A.
CONDEMNED by the COMPAS-SIONATE
10¢
FEATURING...
THE TOWER-KEEPER
THE SAD WITCH
THE CRYPT-LOSER
DONALD J. TRUMP IS CALLING FOR A TOTAL AND COMPLETE SHUTDOWN OF MUSLIMS ENTERING THE UNITED STATES UNTIL OUR COUNTRY'S REPRESENTATIVES CAN FIGURE OUT WHAT THE HELL IS GOING ON.
TIRED
POOR
HUDDLED MASSES

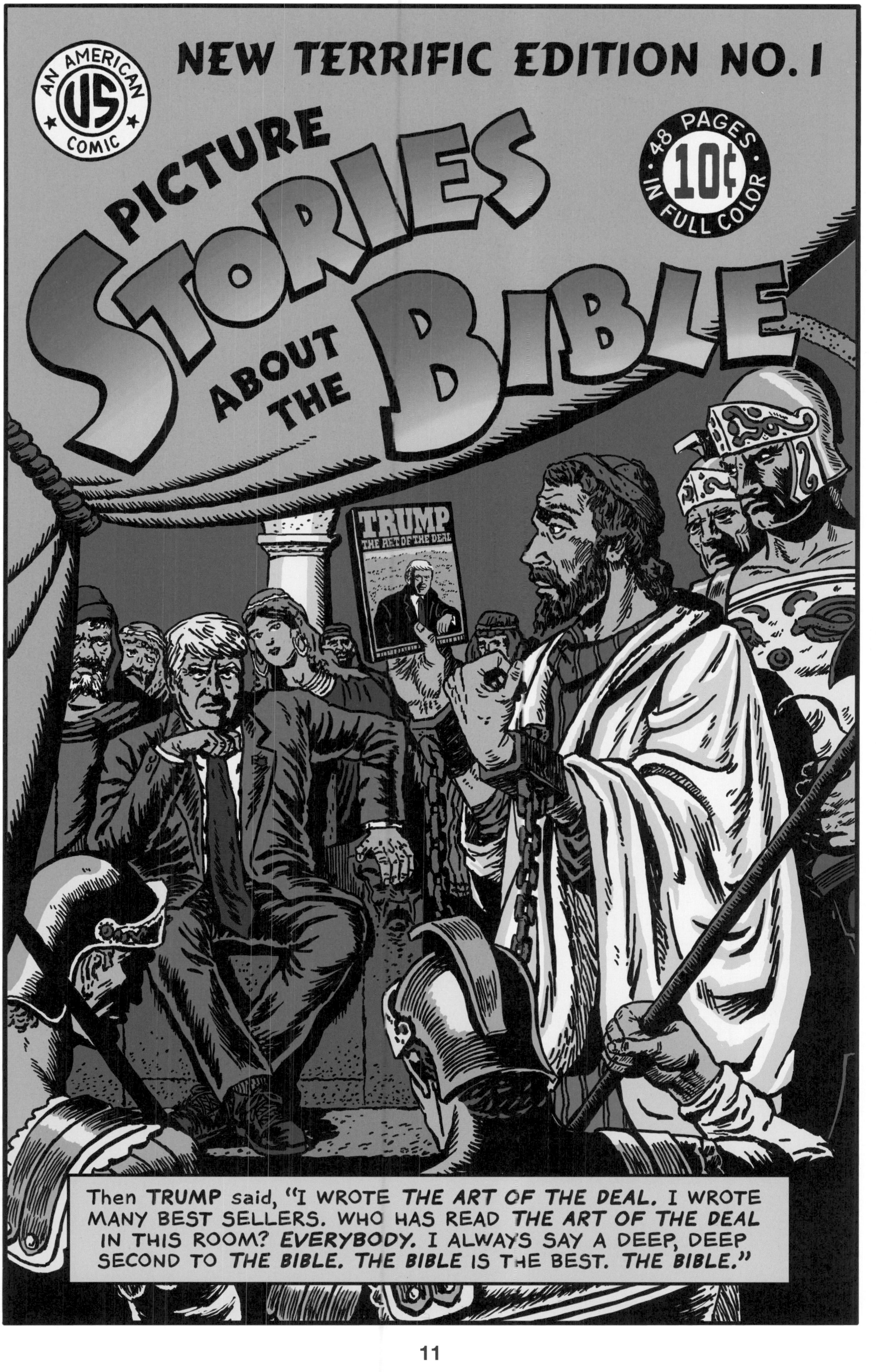
AN AMERICAN US COMIC
NEW TERRIFIC EDITION NO. 1
48 PAGES 10¢ IN FULL COLOR
PICTURE STORIES ABOUT THE BIBLE
TRUMP THE ART OF THE DEAL
Then TRUMP said, "I WROTE THE ART OF THE DEAL. I WROTE MANY BEST SELLERS. WHO HAS READ THE ART OF THE DEAL IN THIS ROOM? EVERYBODY. I ALWAYS SAY A DEEP, DEEP SECOND TO THE BIBLE. THE BIBLE IS THE BEST. THE BIBLE."

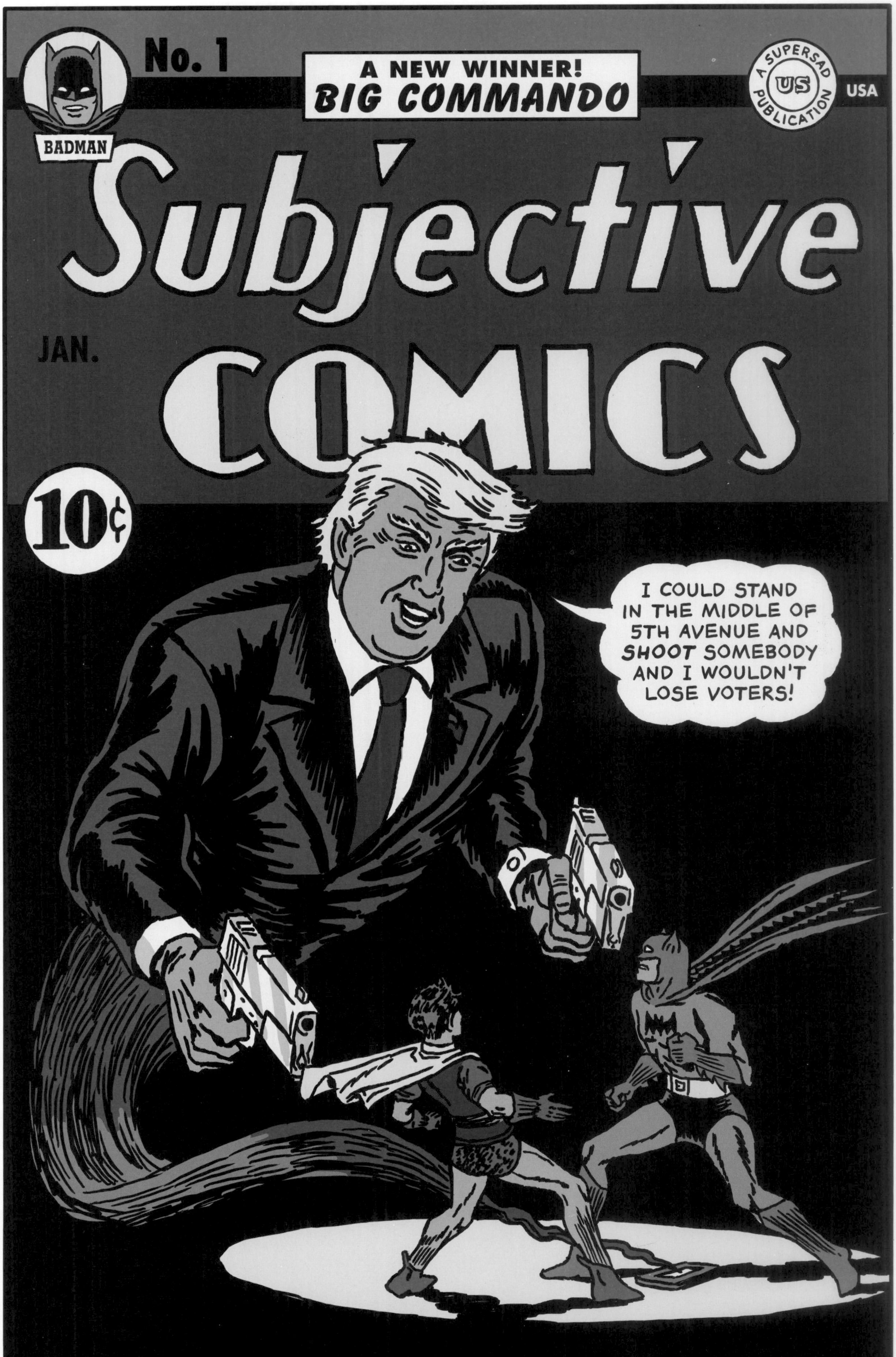
No. 1
A NEW WINNER!
BIG COMMANDO
BADMAN
A SUPERSAD PUBLICATION
US
USA
Subjective
JAN.
COMICS
10¢
I COULD STAND IN THE MIDDLE OF 5TH AVENUE AND SHOOT SOMEBODY AND I WOULDN'T LOSE VOTERS!

GOLD COMIC
02-26-2016
DRUMPFY DON
25¢
DRUMPFY DON
and BAD BUNNY
I'M GOING TO OPEN UP OUR LIBEL LAWS SO WHEN THEY WRITE PURPOSELY NEGATIVE AND HORRIBLE AND FALSE ARTICLES, WE CAN SUE THEM AND WIN LOTS OF MONEY.

IMPACT
AN AMERICAN US COMIC
TRUMP
NO. 1
FEB. 2016
NY ID
10¢
SUSPENSTORIES
I DON'T KNOW ANYTHING ABOUT WHAT YOU'RE EVEN TALKING ABOUT WITH WHITE SUPREMACY OR WHITE SUPREMACISTS.... YOU WOULDN'T WANT ME TO CONDEMN A GROUP THAT I KNOW NOTHING ABOUT.... IF YOU WOULD SEND ME A LIST OF THE GROUPS, I WILL DO RESEARCH ON THEM. AND, CERTAINLY, I WOULD DISAVOW IF I THOUGHT THERE WAS SOMETHING WRONG.

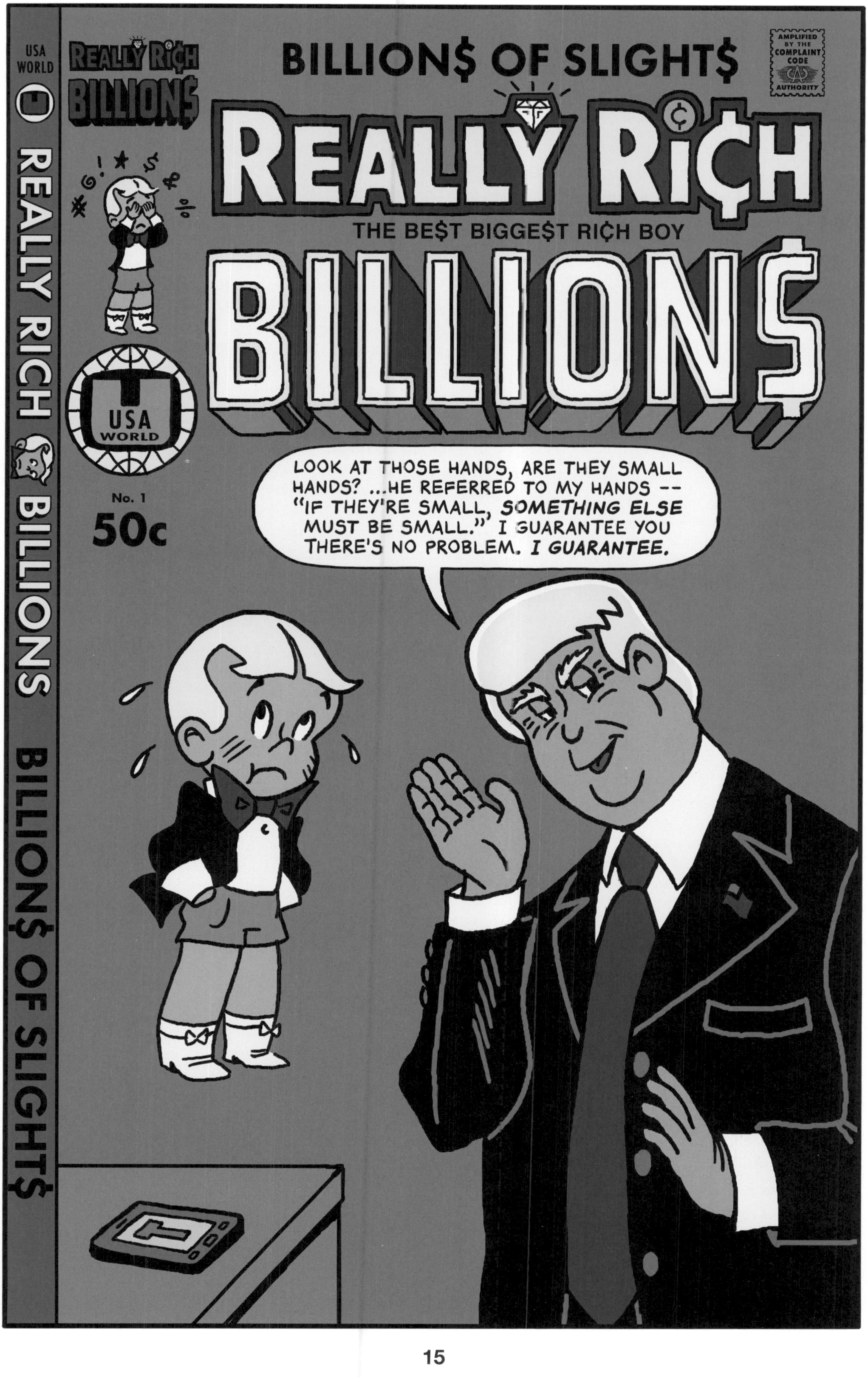
USA WORLD
REALLY RICH BILLIONS
BILLION$ OF SLIGHT$
REALLY RI¢H BILLION$
BILLION$ OF SLIGHT$
AMPLIFIED BY THE COMPLAINT CODE AUTHORITY
REALLY RI¢H
THE BE$T BIGGE$T RI¢H BOY
BILLION$
USA WORLD
No. 1
50c
LOOK AT THOSE HANDS, ARE THEY SMALL HANDS? ...HE REFERRED TO MY HANDS -- "IF THEY'RE SMALL, *SOMETHING ELSE* MUST BE SMALL." I GUARANTEE YOU THERE'S NO PROBLEM. *I GUARANTEE.*

NO. 1
FEB.
only 25¢ Bigger & Best
APPROVED BY THE CONFLICT CODE AUTHORITY
US
JUSTICE WINNERS OF AMERICA?
JUSTICE DEPARTMENT of AMERICA
JUSTICE LOSERS OF AMERICA?
SUPERSAD
FLAK
GREEN LOSER
HAWKSAD
TOM
PLUS
'BEEN
$UPER$@D
FL@K
GR**N LO$ER
H@WK$@D
#OM
+
'%EE#
IF YOU SEE SOMEBODY GETTING READY TO THROW A TOMATO, KNOCK THE CRAP OUT OF THEM...
...JUST KNOCK THE HELL-- I PROMISE YOU, I WILL PAY FOR THE LEGAL FEES.

REELING
FAILING ENTERTAINMENT
DINKY and THE BRAIN
US $1.95
NO.1
MAR 16
US
CONTROLLED BY THE CENTRAL NERVOUS CSN SYSTEM
CLASSY
TREMENDOUS
SMART
TOUGH
TERRIFIC
BIG
RICH
HUGE
BEST
RIGHT
AMAZING
STRONG
I'M SPEAKING WITH MYSELF, NUMBER ONE, BECAUSE I HAVE A VERY GOOD BRAIN AND I'VE SAID A LOT OF THINGS.

'MERICA
COMICS

WE'RE GOING TO **WIN SO MUCH** YOU MAY EVEN GET ***TIRED*** OF WINNING, AND YOU'LL SAY, "PLEASE, PLEASE -- IT'S ***TOO MUCH WINNING.***"

SUPERSAD US NATIONAL NEWS
10¢
MAR. NO. 1
The FLAK
APPROACHED BY THE CONVERSE CODE AUTHORITY
I KNOW WHAT I'M DOING AND I LISTEN TO A LOT OF PEOPLE, I TALK TO A LOT OF PEOPLE AND AT THE APPROPRIATE TIME I'LL TELL YOU WHO THE PEOPLE ARE... BUT MY PRIMARY CONSULTANT IS MYSELF AND I HAVE A GOOD INSTINCT FOR THIS STUFF.

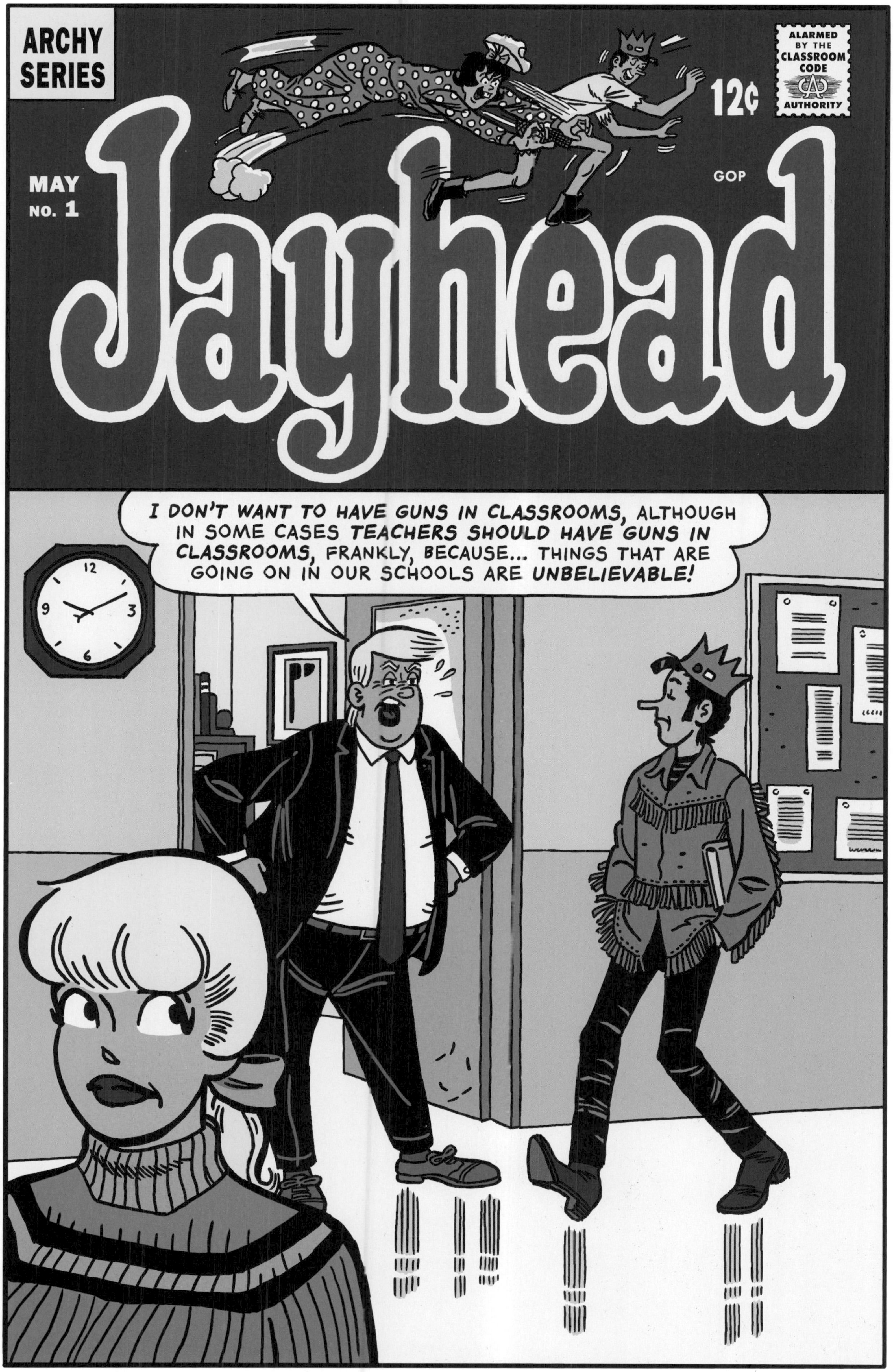
ARCHY SERIES
12¢
ALARMED BY THE CLASSROOM CODE AUTHORITY
MAY NO. 1
GOP
Jayhead
I DON'T WANT TO HAVE GUNS IN CLASSROOMS, ALTHOUGH IN SOME CASES TEACHERS SHOULD HAVE GUNS IN CLASSROOMS, FRANKLY, BECAUSE... THINGS THAT ARE GOING ON IN OUR SCHOOLS ARE UNBELIEVABLE!

MASTER OF THE ATMOSPHERIC ARTS!
DOCTOR SCIENCE
'MERICA COMICS GROUP
12¢ IND.
1 JAN
QUESTIONED BY THE CARBON CODE AUTHORITY
I THINK THE CLIMATE CHANGE IS JUST A VERY, VERY EXPENSIVE FORM OF TAX. A LOT OF PEOPLE ARE MAKING A LOT OF MONEY.... BUT THIS IS DONE FOR THE BENEFIT OF CHINA, BECAUSE CHINA DOES NOT DO ANYTHING TO HELP CLIMATE CHANGE. THEY BURN EVERYTHING YOU COULD BURN; THEY COULDN'T CARE LESS.... SO IT'S VERY HARD ON OUR BUSINESS.

EL CÓMIC
JULY NO. 1
Still 10¢
Little Flunky
TODAY IS THE BEST EVIDENCE EVER THAT WE'VE SEEN THAT OUR SYSTEM IS ABSOLUTELY, TOTALLY RIGGED!

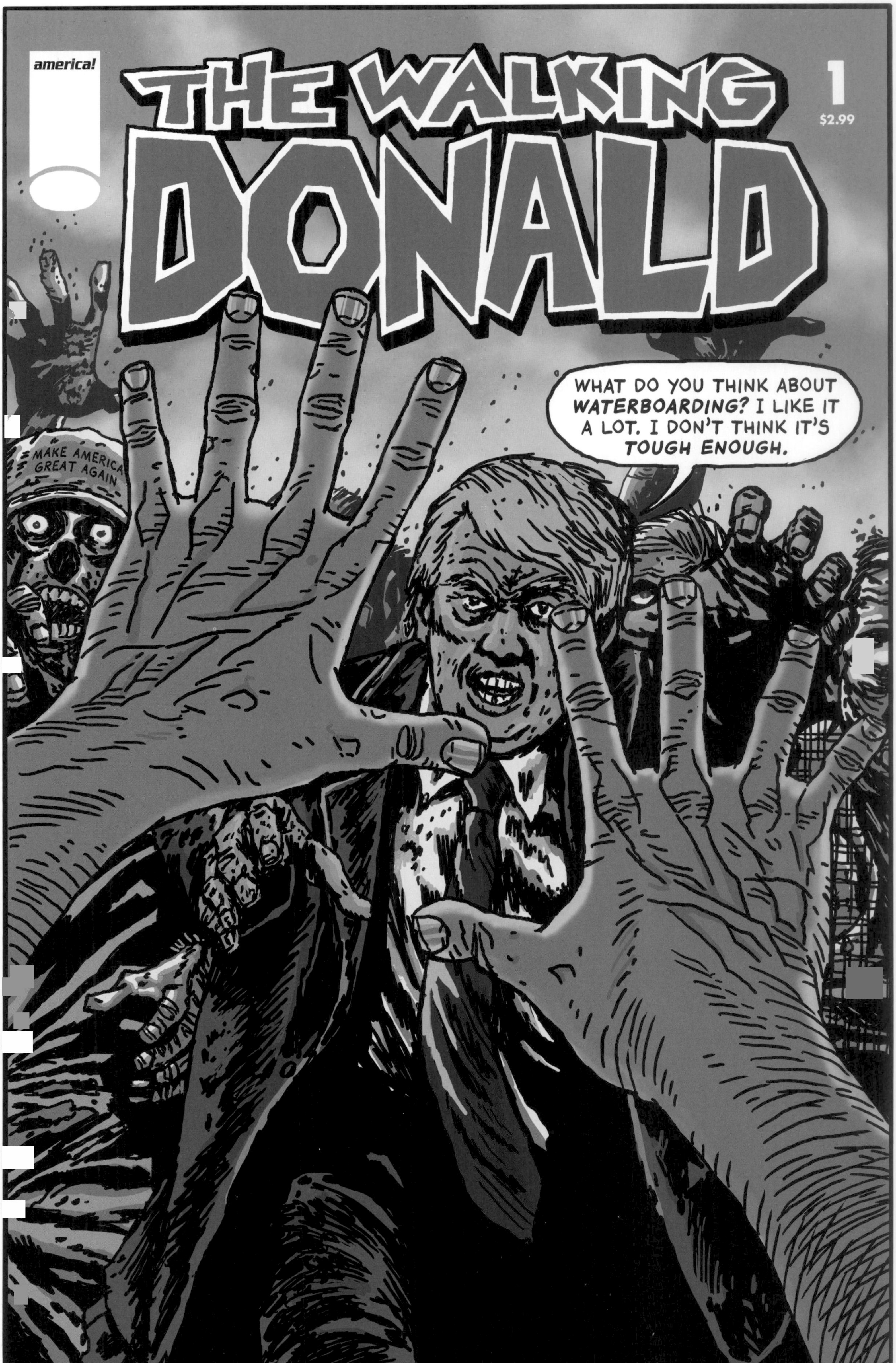
america!
THE WALKING DONALD
1
$2.99
MAKE AMERICA GREAT AGAIN
WHAT DO YOU THINK ABOUT WATERBOARDING? I LIKE IT A LOT. I DON'T THINK IT'S TOUGH ENOUGH.

usa boom!
ADVERSARY TIME
#1
I have a message to every last person threatening the peace on our streets and the safety of our police: WHEN I TAKE THE OATH OF OFFICE NEXT YEAR, I WILL RESTORE LAW AND ORDER TO OUR COUNTRY.
BMO

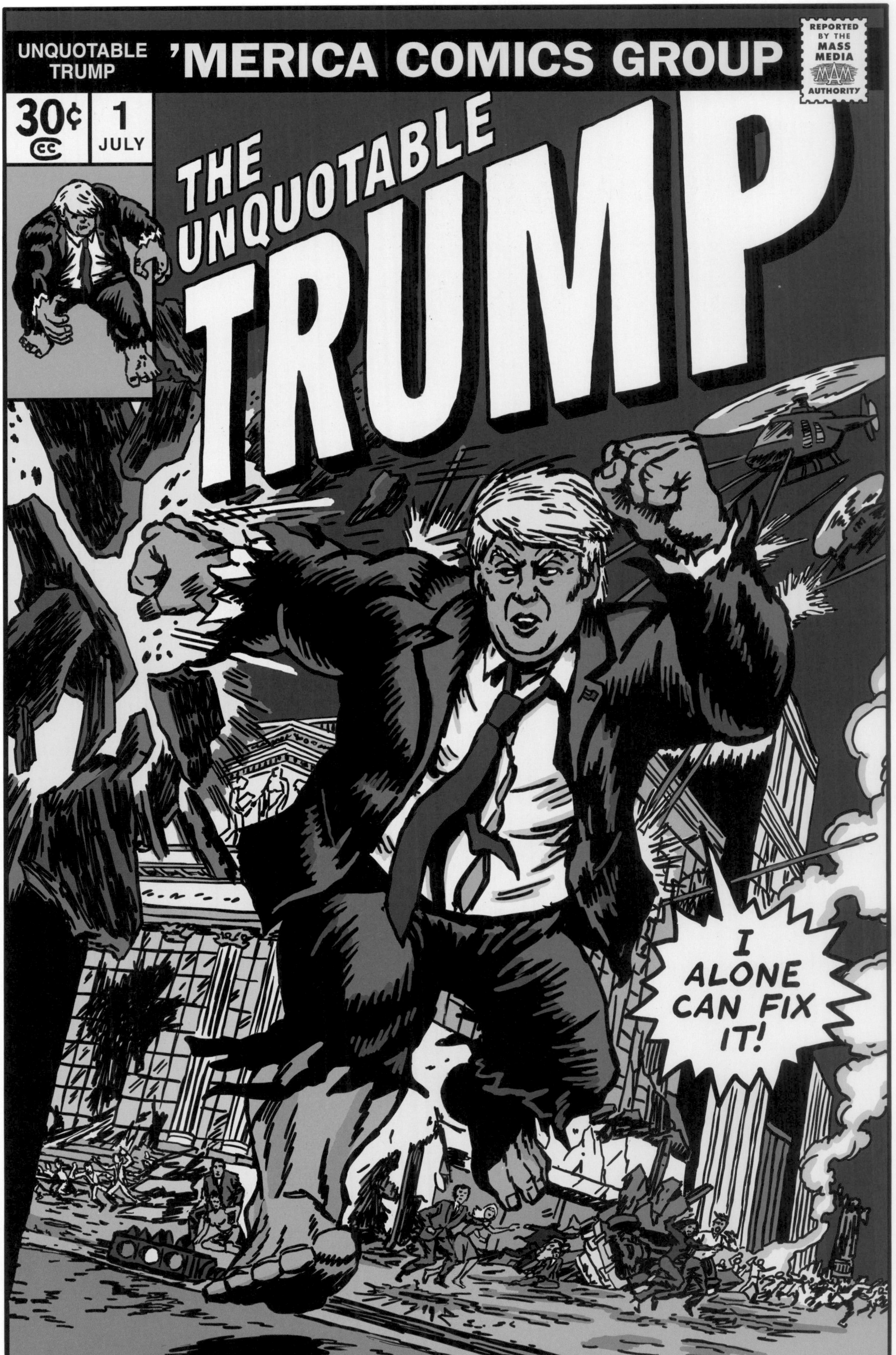
UNQUOTABLE TRUMP
'MERICA COMICS GROUP
REPORTED BY THE MASS MEDIA AUTHORITY
30¢
1
JULY
THE UNQUOTABLE TRUMP
I ALONE CAN FIX IT!

'MERICA
#1 IN A MULTI-ISSUE UNLIMITED SERIES
'MERICA SUPER LOSERS
PUBLIC WARS
75¢ U.S.A. M 1 AUG
SOMETIMES IN THE HEAT OF DEBATE... YOU DON'T CHOOSE THE RIGHT WORDS OR YOU SAY THE WRONG THING. I HAVE DONE THAT.
AND BELIEVE IT OR NOT, I REGRET IT. ...PARTICULARLY WHERE IT MAY HAVE CAUSED PERSONAL PAIN.
TOO MUCH IS AT STAKE FOR US TO BE CONSUMED WITH THESE ISSUES.
BUT ONE THING; I CAN PROMISE YOU THIS: I WILL ALWAYS TELL YOU THE TRUTH.

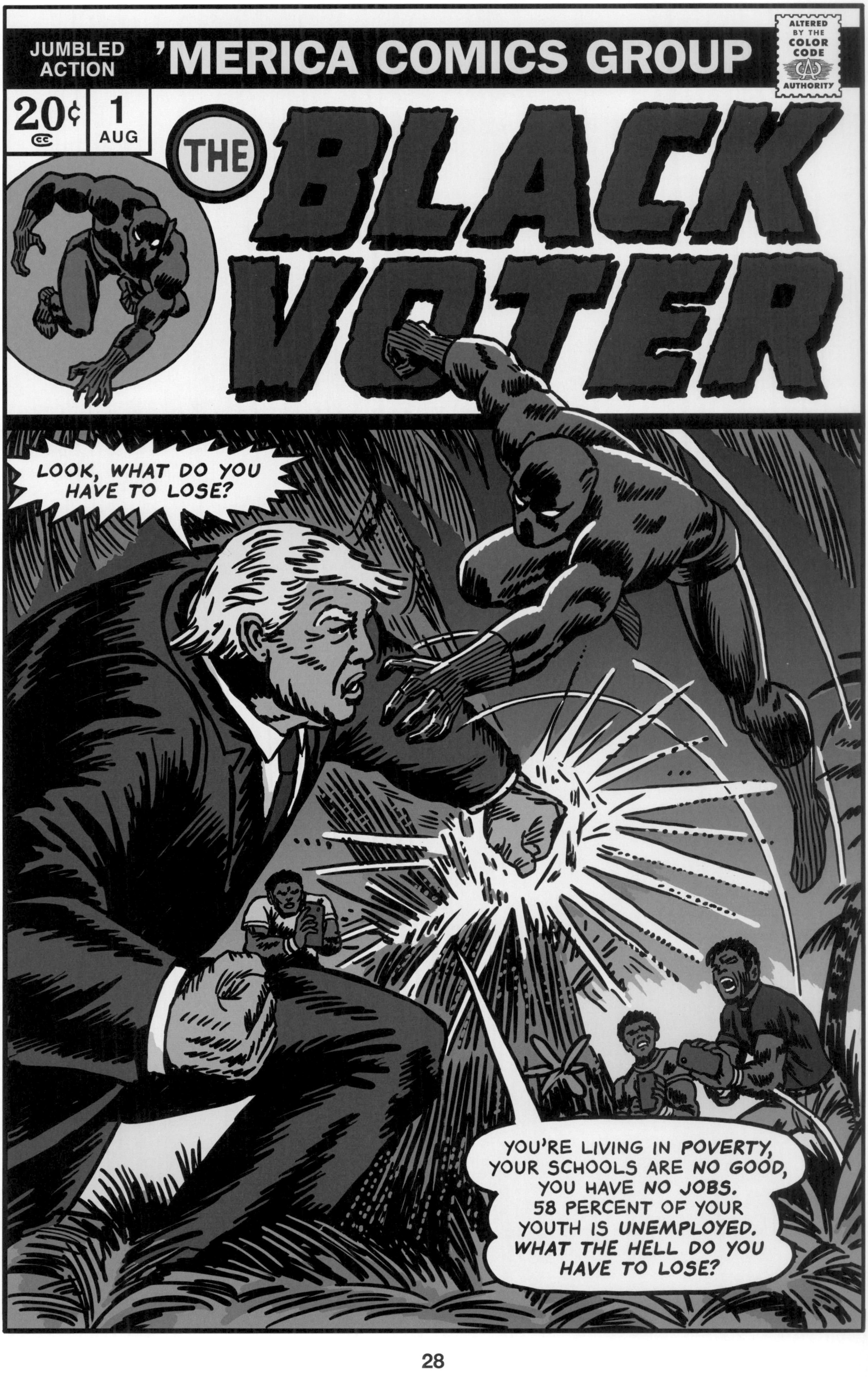
JUMBLED ACTION
'MERICA COMICS GROUP
ALTERED BY THE COLOR CODE AUTHORITY
20¢
1 AUG
THE BLACK VOTER
LOOK, WHAT DO YOU HAVE TO LOSE?
YOU'RE LIVING IN POVERTY, YOUR SCHOOLS ARE NO GOOD, YOU HAVE NO JOBS. 58 PERCENT OF YOUR YOUTH IS UNEMPLOYED. WHAT THE HELL DO YOU HAVE TO LOSE?

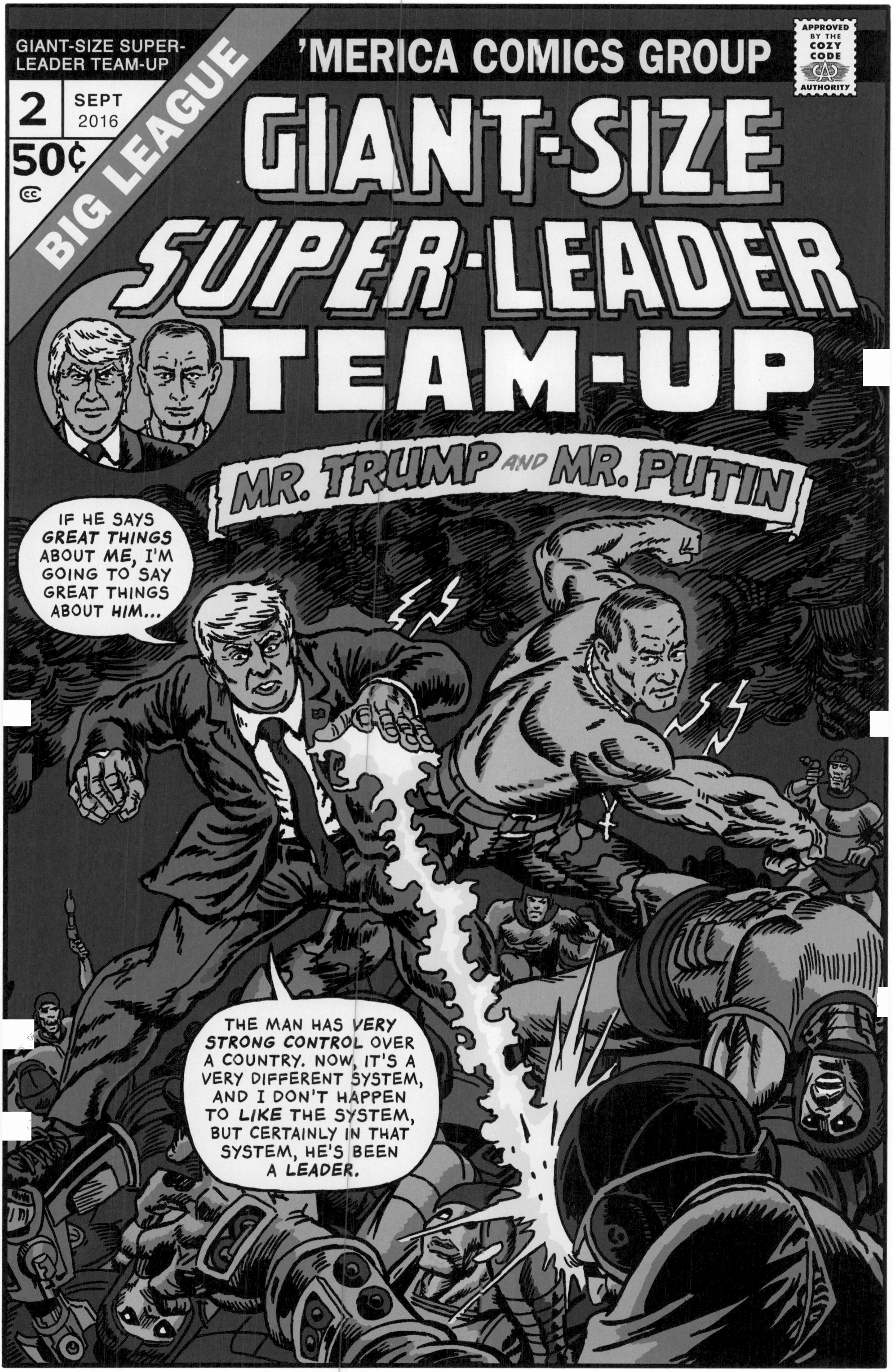
GIANT-SIZE SUPER-LEADER TEAM-UP
2
SEPT 2016
50¢
BIG LEAGUE
'MERICA COMICS GROUP
APPROVED BY THE COZY CODE AUTHORITY
GIANT-SIZE SUPER-LEADER TEAM-UP
MR. TRUMP AND MR. PUTIN
IF HE SAYS GREAT THINGS ABOUT ME, I'M GOING TO SAY GREAT THINGS ABOUT HIM...
THE MAN HAS VERY STRONG CONTROL OVER A COUNTRY. NOW, IT'S A VERY DIFFERENT SYSTEM, AND I DON'T HAPPEN TO LIKE THE SYSTEM, BUT CERTAINLY IN THAT SYSTEM, HE'S BEEN A LEADER.

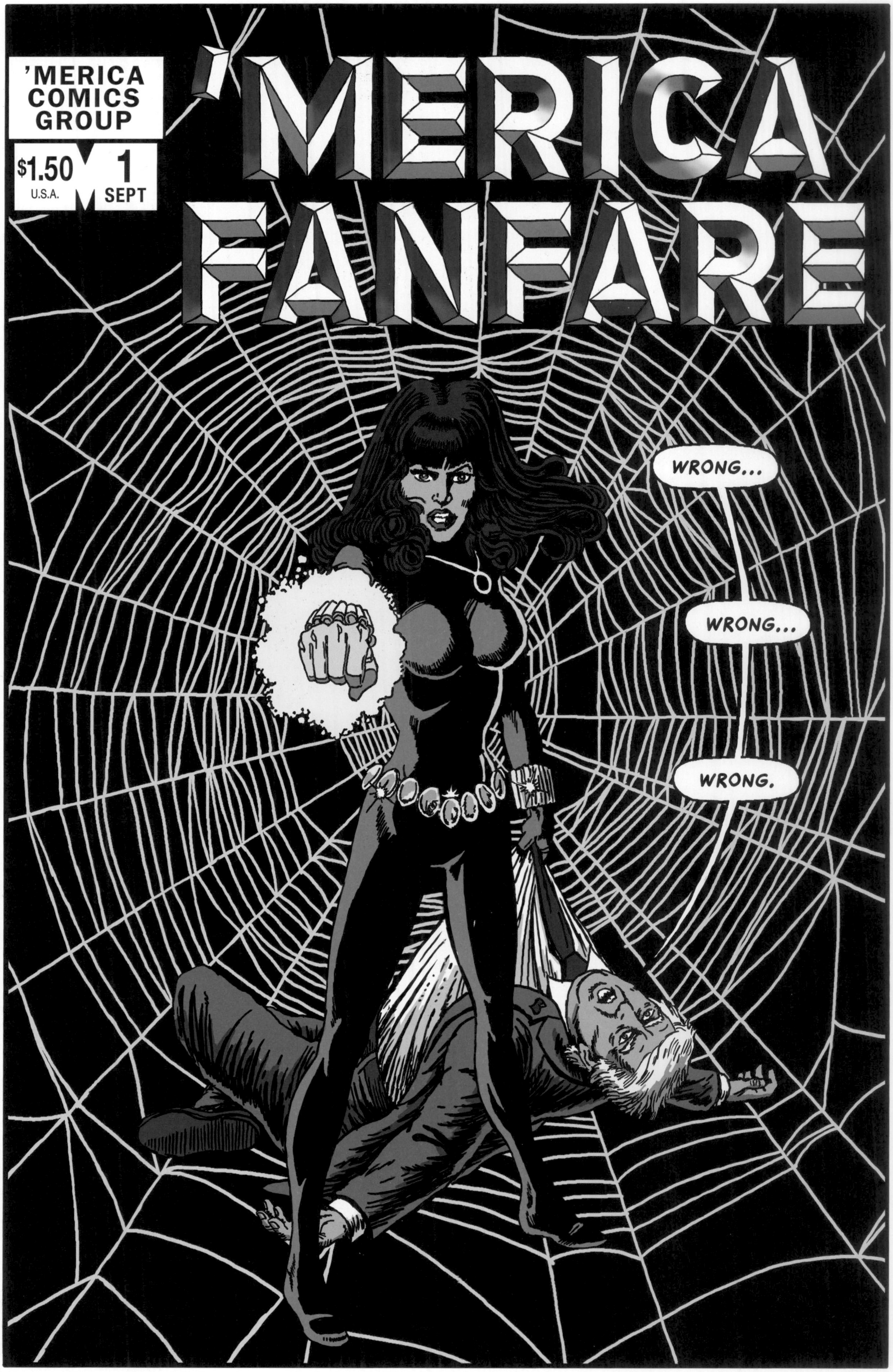
'MERICA COMICS GROUP
$1.50 U.S.A.
1 SEPT
'MERICA FANFARE
WRONG...
WRONG...
WRONG.

US
cat pussy
1 OCT
QUESTIONED BY THE CONTEMPT CODE AUTHORITY
NOBODY HAS MORE RESPECT FOR WOMEN THAN I DO.

AMERICA'S BADDEST COMIC MAGAZINE!
HOMBRES FANTÁSTICOS
12¢ IND.
1 OCT
OVERLOOKED BY THE CONSTRUCTION CODE AUTHORITY
Hombres Fantásticos
'MERICA COMICS GROUP
WE HAVE SOME BAD, BAD PEOPLE IN THIS COUNTRY THAT HAVE TO GO OUT....
AND ONCE THE BORDER IS SECURED AT A LATER DATE, WE'LL MAKE A DETERMINATION AS TO THE REST.
THE WALL!

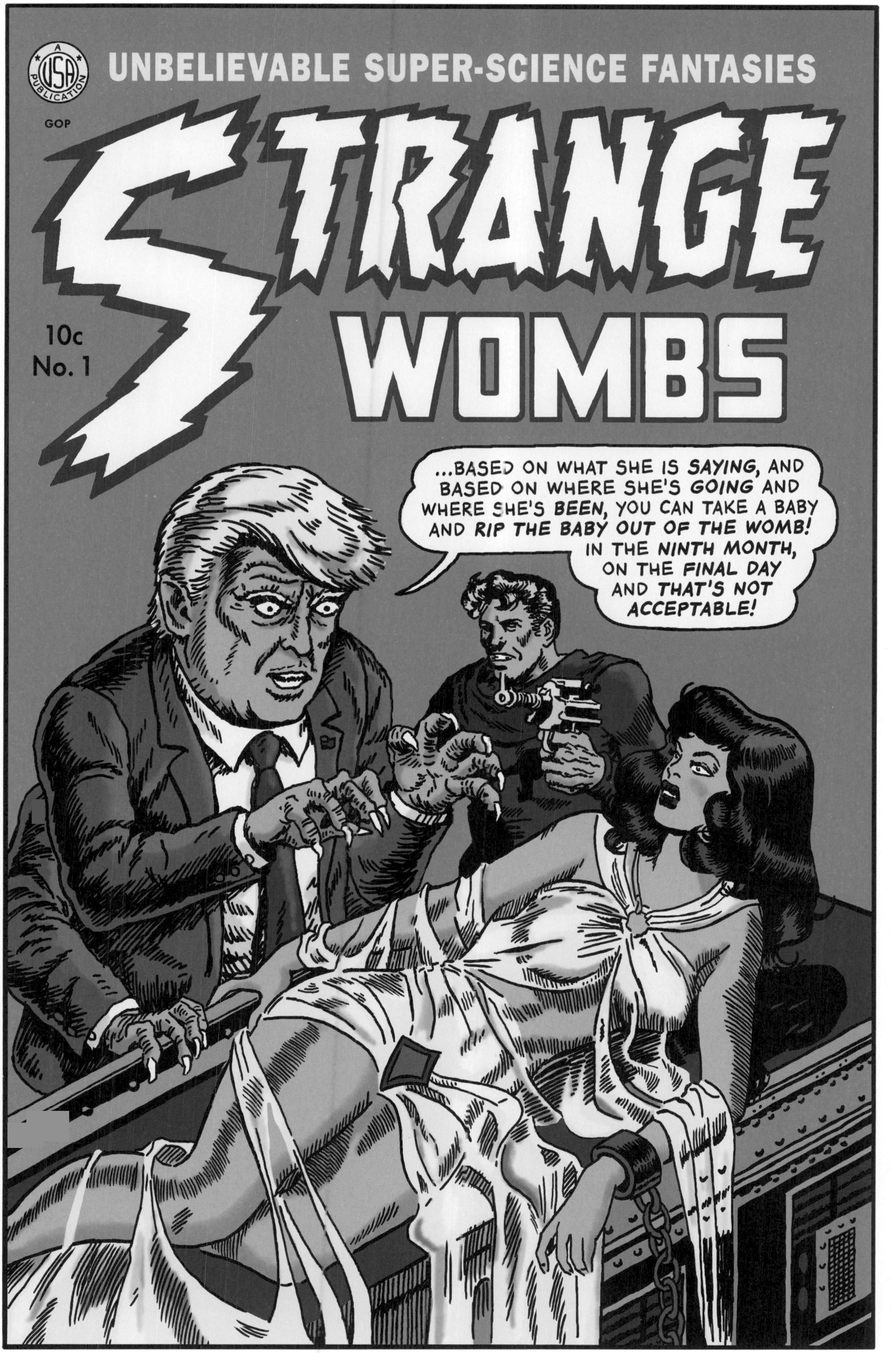

A USA PUBLICATION
GOP
UNBELIEVABLE SUPER-SCIENCE FANTASIES
STRANGE WOMBS
10c
No. 1
...BASED ON WHAT SHE IS SAYING, AND BASED ON WHERE SHE'S GOING AND WHERE SHE'S BEEN, YOU CAN TAKE A BABY AND RIP THE BABY OUT OF THE WOMB! IN THE NINTH MONTH, ON THE FINAL DAY AND THAT'S NOT ACCEPTABLE!

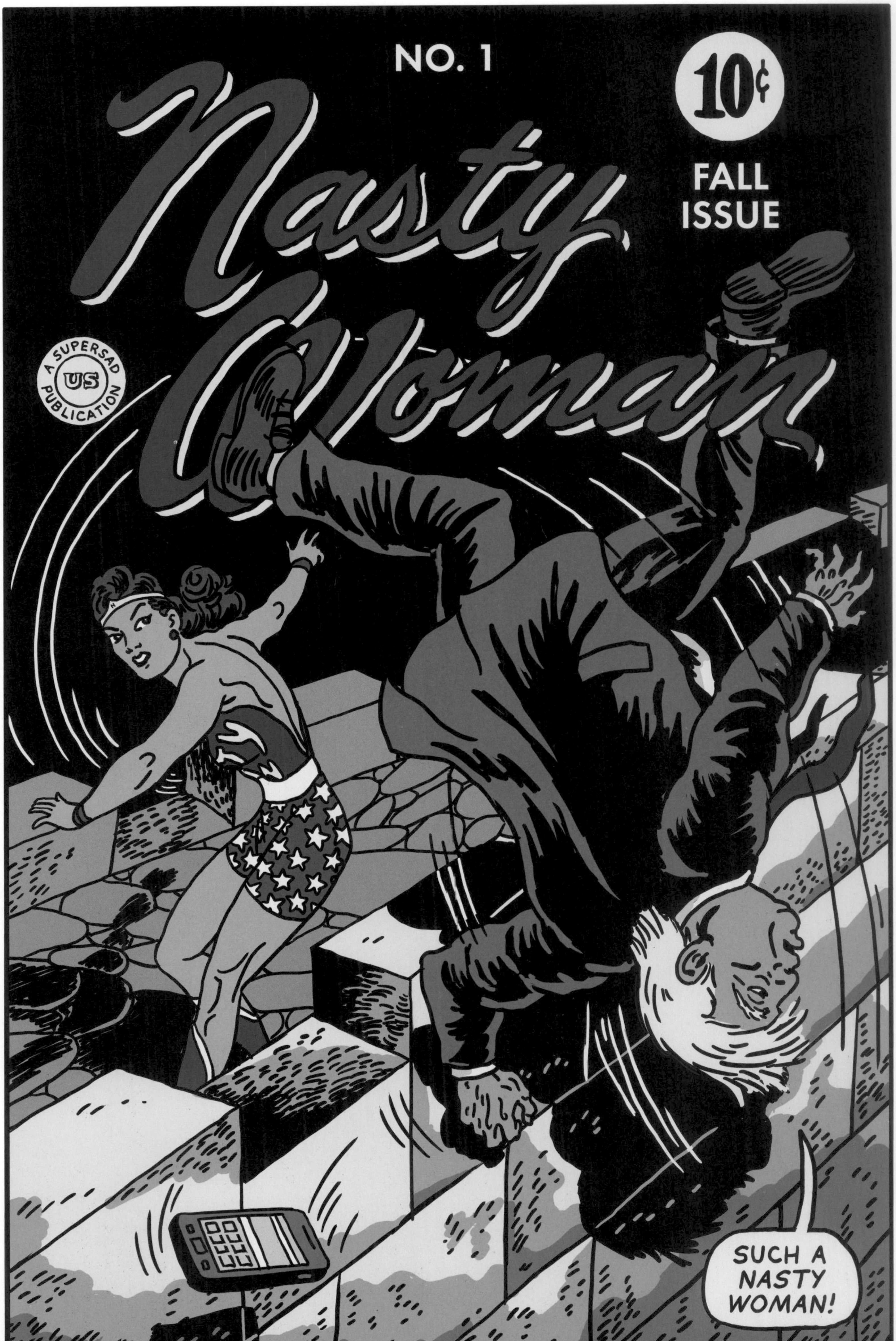
NO. 1
Nasty Woman
10¢
FALL ISSUE
A SUPERSAD US PUBLICATION
SUCH A NASTY WOMAN!

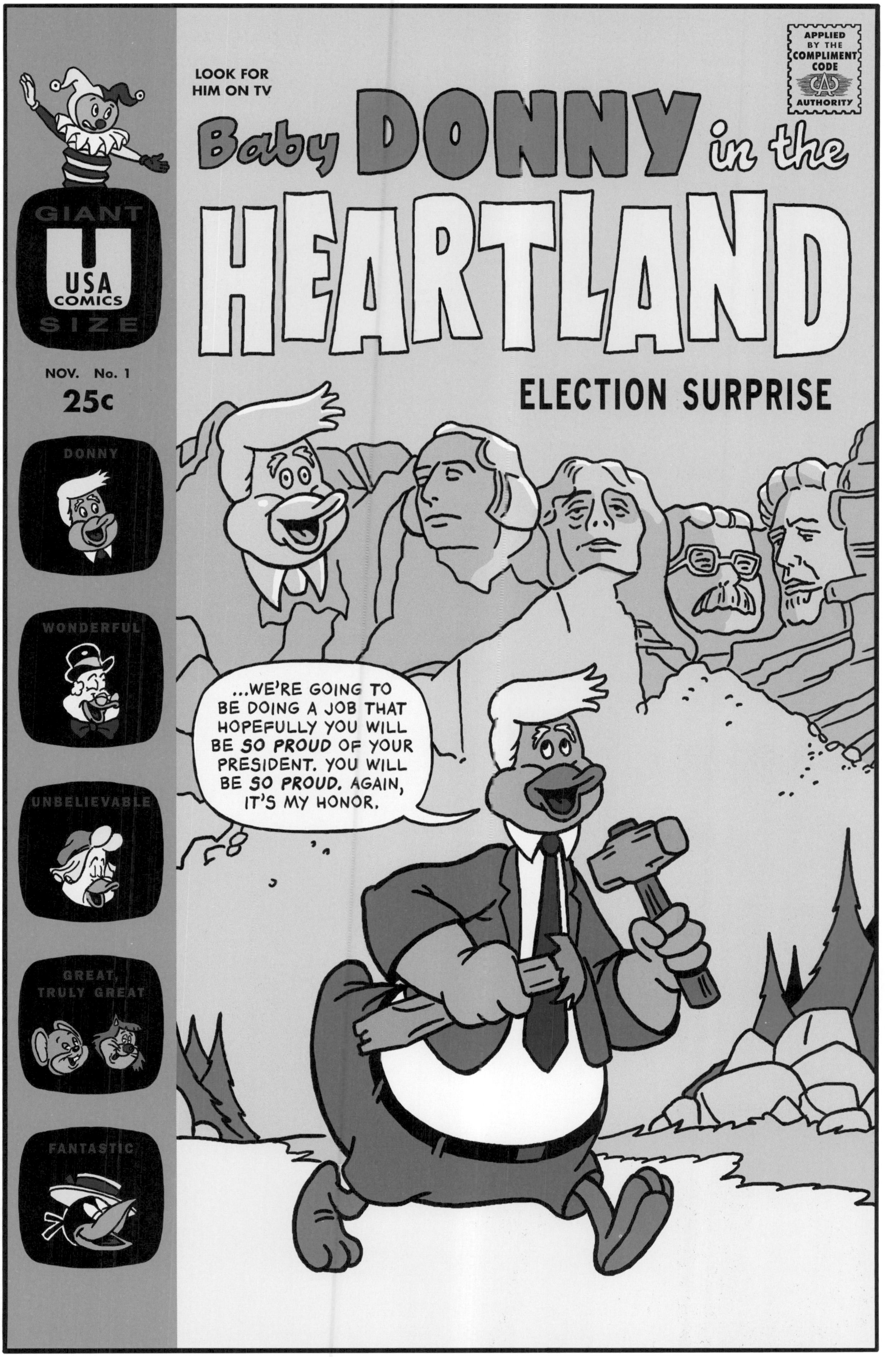

APPLIED BY THE COMPLIMENT CODE AUTHORITY
LOOK FOR HIM ON TV
Baby DONNY in the HEARTLAND
GIANT U USA COMICS SIZE
NOV. No. 1
25¢
ELECTION SURPRISE
DONNY
WONDERFUL
UNBELIEVABLE
GREAT, TRULY GREAT
FANTASTIC
...WE'RE GOING TO BE DOING A JOB THAT HOPEFULLY YOU WILL BE SO PROUD OF YOUR PRESIDENT. YOU WILL BE SO PROUD. AGAIN, IT'S MY HONOR.

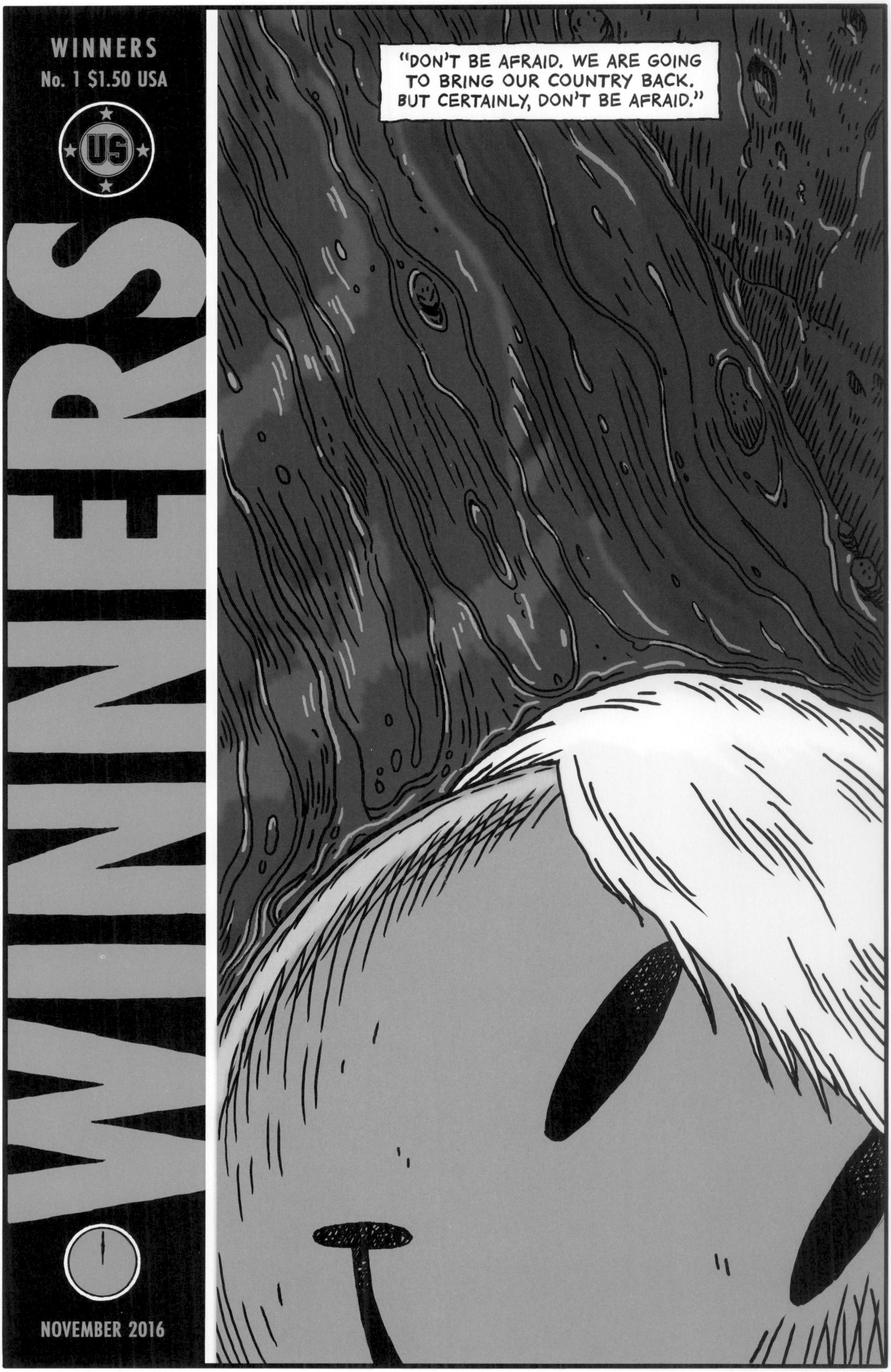
WINNERS
No. 1 $1.50 USA
US
WINNERS
NOVEMBER 2016
"DON'T BE AFRAID. WE ARE GOING TO BRING OUR COUNTRY BACK. BUT CERTAINLY, DON'T BE AFRAID."

SUPERSAD US NATIONAL NEWS
10¢ Extra! Extra!
JAN. NO. 1
RESEARCHED BY THE FACT-CHECK CODE AUTHORITY
SUPERSAD
DAILY PLAIN
YOU KNOW, I'VE BEEN HEARING MORE AND MORE ABOUT A THING CALLED FAKE NEWS AND THEY'RE TALKING ABOUT PEOPLE THAT GO AND SAY ALL SORTS OF THINGS.
BUT I WILL TELL YOU, SOME OF THE MEDIA OUTLETS THAT I DEAL WITH ARE FAKE NEWS MORE SO THAN ANYBODY.
SAD

GOLD COMIC
UNCLE TRUMP
STILL ONLY 12¢
America's UNCLE TRUMP
11-2017
JANUARY
YOU KNOW, THE ONLY ONE THAT CARES ABOUT MY TAX RETURNS ARE THE REPORTERS, OK? THEY'RE THE ONLY ONES.

'MERICA COMICS
TRUMPUS
THE PRESIDENT
#1
$3.50
APPROVED BY THE ELECTORAL COLLEGE EA AUTHORITY
THIS AMERICAN CARNAGE STOPS RIGHT HERE AND STOPS RIGHT NOW!

THE BIG INAUGURATION
SIN-CERE
GOD LOOKED DOWN AND HE SAID, "WE'RE NOT GOING TO LET IT RAIN ON YOUR SPEECH..."
THE FIRST LINE, I GOT HIT BY A COUPLE OF DROPS. AND I SAID, "OH, THIS IS TOO BAD..."
BUT THE TRUTH IS THAT IT STOPPED IMMEDIATELY. IT WAS AMAZING. AND THEN IT BECAME REALLY SUNNY.

WORLD'S FAILEST
COMICS
US WORLD'S FAILEST
15¢
presents
NO. 1
JAN.
EXHAUSTED BY THE CLIMATE CODE AUTHORITY
SUPERSAD and AQUASAD
I AM TO A LARGE EXTENT AN ENVIRONMENTALIST.
I BELIEVE IN IT, BUT IT'S OUT OF CONTROL!

1 of ALL
$2.95 US
DARK ARTS COMICS
...WHAT'S GOING ON WITH VOTER FRAUD IS HORRIBLE. THAT'S NUMBER ONE. NUMBER TWO, I WOULD'VE WON THE POPULAR VOTE IF I WAS CAMPAIGNING FOR THE POPULAR VOTE.
...I WOULD'VE GONE TO A COUPLE OF PLACES THAT I DIDN'T GO TO. AND I WOULD'VE WON THAT MUCH EASIER THAN WINNING THE ELECTORAL COLLEGE.
...BUT IT TURNED OUT I DIDN'T NEED IT BECAUSE WE ENDED UP WINNING BY A MASSIVE AMOUNT, 306. I NEEDED 270. WE GOT 306.

306
ELECTORAL
VOTES

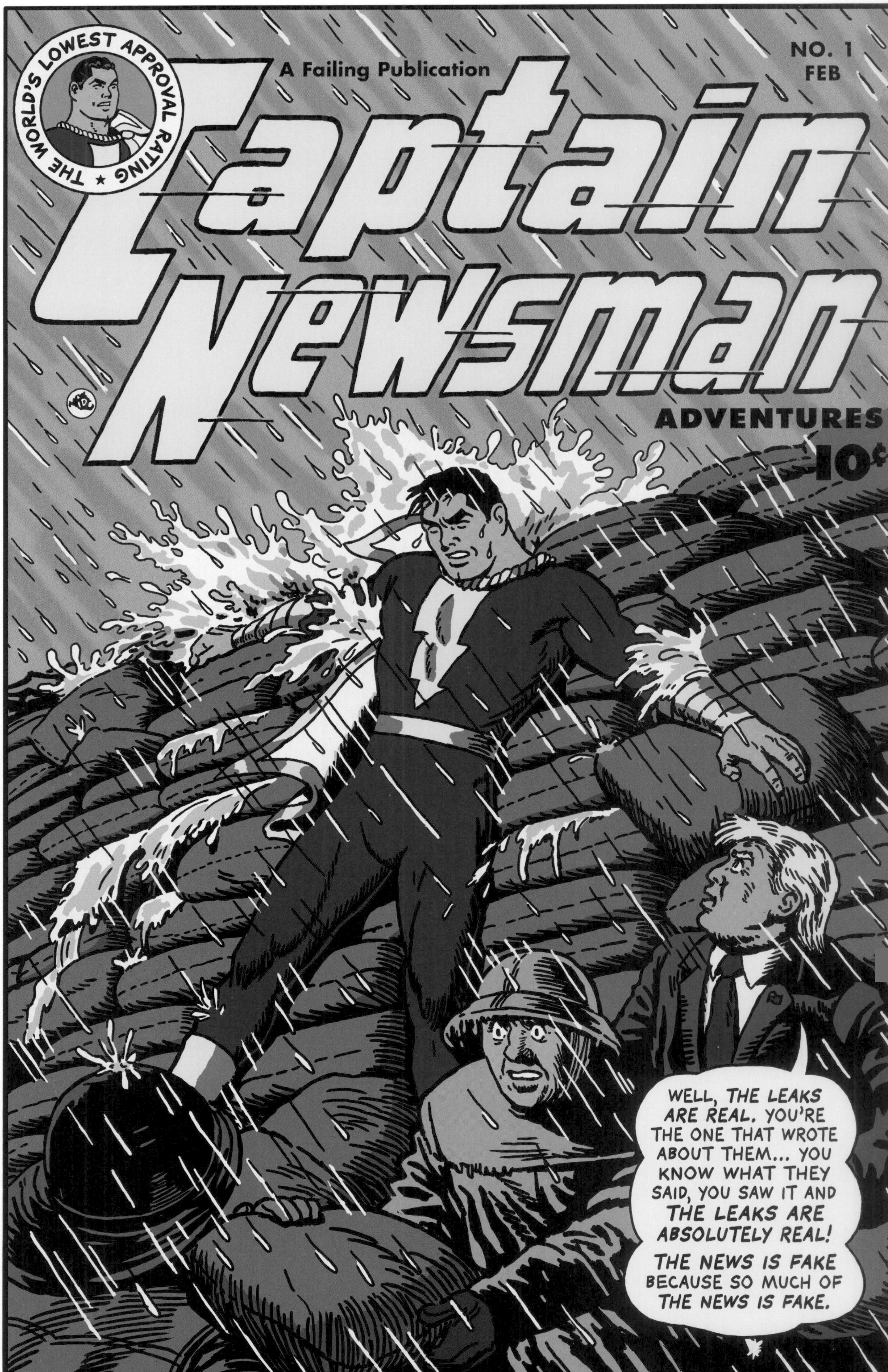
THE WORLD'S LOWEST APPROVAL RATING
A Failing Publication
NO. 1
FEB
Captain Newsman
ADVENTURES
10¢
WELL, THE LEAKS ARE REAL. YOU'RE THE ONE THAT WROTE ABOUT THEM... YOU KNOW WHAT THEY SAID, YOU SAW IT AND THE LEAKS ARE ABSOLUTELY REAL!
THE NEWS IS FAKE BECAUSE SO MUCH OF THE NEWS IS FAKE.

PAWN
america!
1 FEB
$1.95 USA
TOMORROW, THEY WILL SAY, "DONALD TRUMP RANTS AND RAVES AT THE PRESS." I'M NOT RANTING AND RAVING. I'M JUST TELLING YOU.
YOU KNOW, YOU'RE DISHONEST PEOPLE. BUT I'M NOT RANTING AND RAVING. I LOVE THIS. I'M HAVING A GOOD TIME DOING IT.

AILING NOVELTIES
UNITED STATES COMIC BOOK CO.
50¢
Mr. Unfair
VERY, VERY UNFAIR!

#1
usa boom!
D.T. NUTS
I THINK THAT YOU'RE GOING TO SEE A LOT OF DIFFERENT UNITED STATES OF AMERICA OVER THE NEXT THREE, FOUR, OR EIGHT YEARS. I THINK A LOT OF GOOD THINGS ARE HAPPENING AND YOU'RE GOING TO SEE A LOT OF LOVE.

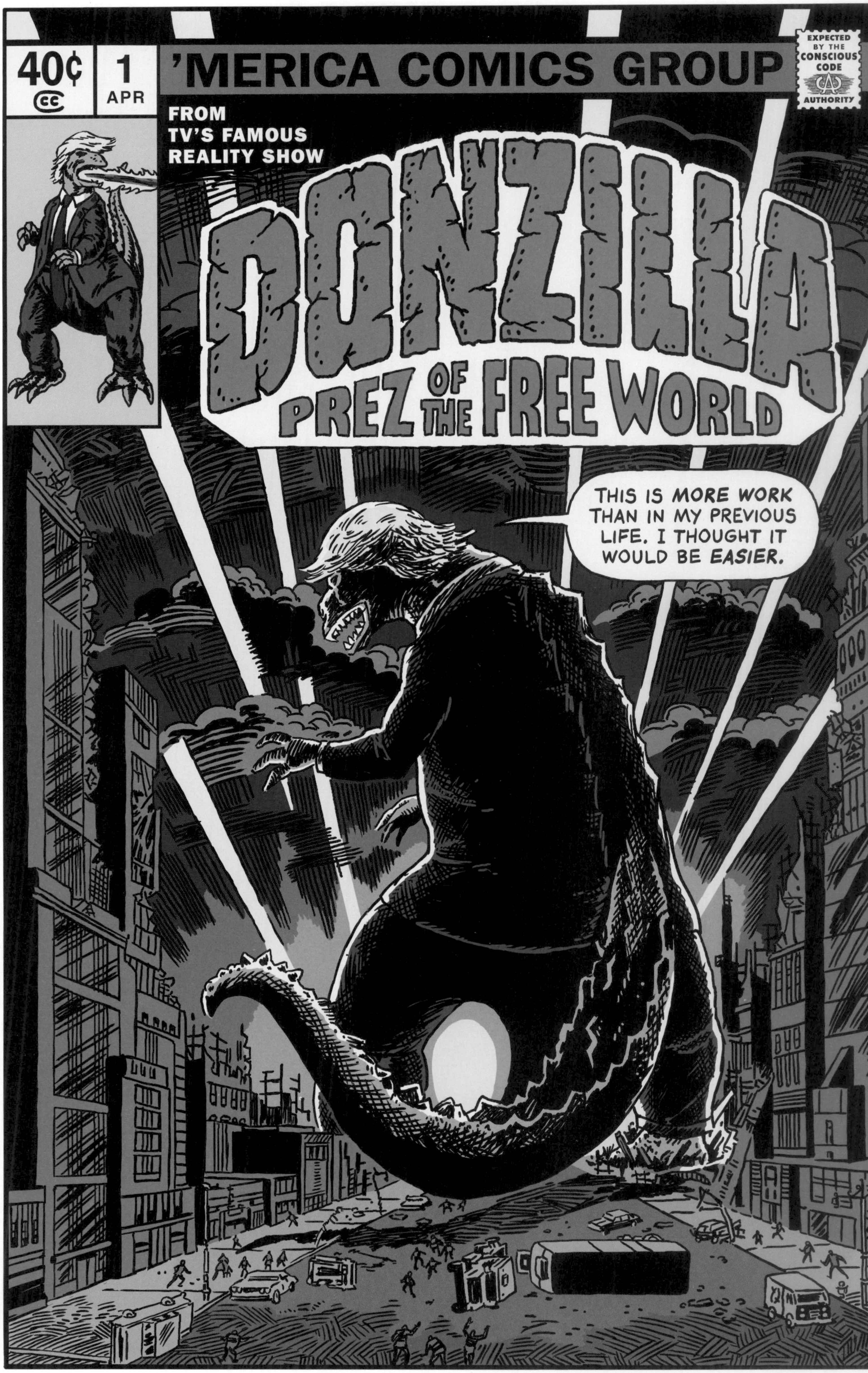
40¢
CC
1
APR
'MERICA COMICS GROUP
EXPECTED BY THE CONSCIOUS CODE AUTHORITY
FROM TV'S FAMOUS REALITY SHOW
DONZILLA
PREZ OF THE FREE WORLD
THIS IS MORE WORK THAN IN MY PREVIOUS LIFE. I THOUGHT IT WOULD BE EASIER.